Bobby's Purple Shoes

...a true story

Written and Illustrated by
Linda Oberlin

Bobby's Purple Shoes

Photography by Lori Hetherington

ISBN 978-0-9911382-3-4

Little Worm Publishing

to Bobby

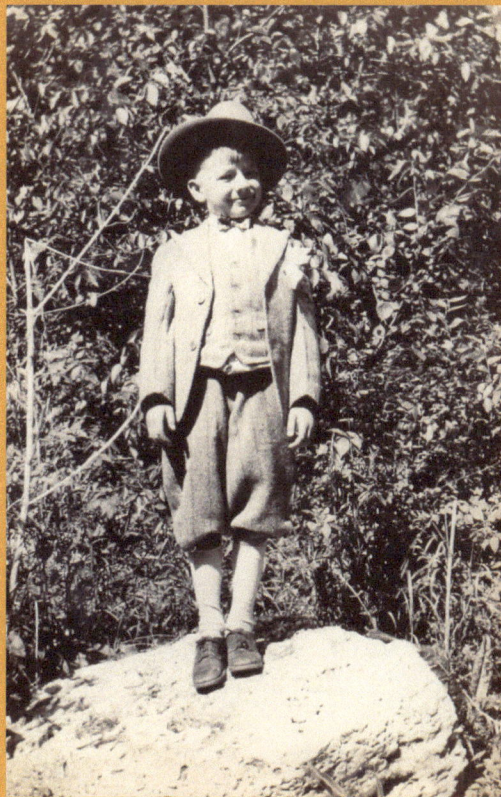

It was 1936
and many people were poor.

Bobby's 12 year old frame
stood small at the door.

He lived in an apartment
called a cold water flat,

With his mother and father
a sister and cat.

Their home wasn't fancy
but it was nice compared to a lot.

Bobby slept by the stove
in the kitchen on a cot.

School would start soon
and Fall was in the air.

Bobby's clothes and his socks
were in need of repair.

With a stitch here and there
his mother could sew.

Bobby's shirt needs a button,
patch his socks at the toe.

These were mends
his mother could make

but the condition of his shoes
were not something they could fake.

The size was too small
and the top had left the sole.

Water could leak in
the large gaping hole.

So off to the store
Mother and Bobby went.

Although he was excited
a lot of money wouldn't be spent.

All the shoes
were lined up in a row,

Like shiny leather beacons
smiling toe to toe.

At the end of the line
was a remarkable sight.

A beautiful pair,
except they were....WHITE!

"Some polish of black
should do nicely.

I'll give you a fair price,"
said the store clerk politely.

The pair of shoes were boxed
Mother and Bobby left the store.

They waved good-bye
As they hurried out the door.

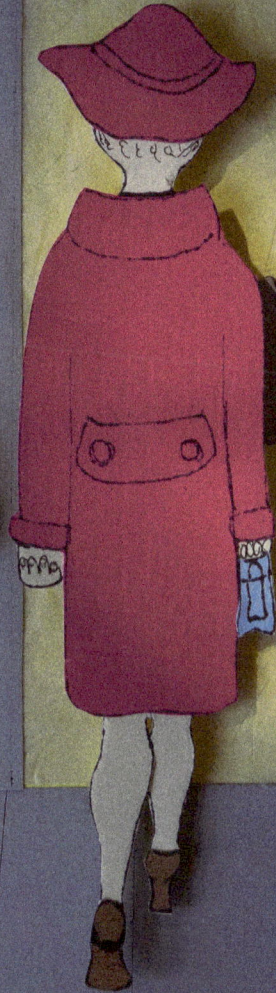

Sunday afternoon
Mother scrubbed and polished
and took extra care,

to cover all the white with black
and dry in the warm air.

Much to Bobby's surprise
the shoes turned PURPLE...not BLACK!

It was Monday, school was in an hour
there was no turning back!

As he dressed for the first day
his clothes were clean and neat.

But Bobby couldn't help
but stare at his own feet.

With an oversized hat
and britches at one knee,

he felt small and afraid,
that was plain to see.

The lonely walk to school
was filled with dismay.

The kids were sure to tease him
on this very long first day.

He stood at the front steps
feeling nervous, sick, and full of dread.

He just wanted to run home
and go back to bed!

The bell rang...doors were shut...
he would be brave and face them all.

Slowly, with a heavy heart,
he made his way down the long lonely hall.

Bobby stood at the teacher's desk
feeling timid and shy.

The hush in the room and all the blank stares
made him feel as though he could cry.

But the silence was broken
when a student shouted out to all,

"Hooray! Bobby is here!
Now we have a team for baseball!"

By the end of the day
Bobby had forgotten his purple shoes.

What anyone was wearing
had become old news.

As the years passed by
his shoes were outgrown.

Bobby became a soldier, a husband,
and had a family of his own.

But after many many years
Bobby would always remember,

friends that were kind and accepting
with a polite and mild temper.

So, if you want to be remembered
and not sure what attitude to choose...

Just remember the story
of Bobby's Purple Shoes.

www.ingramcontent.com/pod-product-compliance
Lightning Source LLC
Chambersburg PA
CBHW042115040426

42449CB00002B/54